THIS BOOK MAY BE KEPT

FO N DAYS

A
day

This Book may

URTEEN

One Cent is
ok is overdue
r deposit st
n, Fi
the b

MAY 3

AB

RAHAM LINCOLN

AN INITIAL BIOGRAPHY

BY

GENEVIEVE FOSTER

CHARLES SCRIBNER'S SONS · NEW YORK

[illegible] LIBRARY 93223

COPYRIGHT 1950 BY
GENEVIEVE FOSTER

PRINTED IN THE UNITED STATES OF AMERICA

ALL RIGHTS RESERVED. NO PART OF THIS BOOK
MAY BE REPRODUCED IN ANY FORM WITHOUT
THE PERMISSION OF CHARLES SCRIBNER'S SONS

A

9/1/51 Samm[illegible]

1809

KENTUCKY

It was a frosty February morning in the year 1809. A small boy in buckskin breeches and a coonskin cap, was running as fast as he could go along a narrow backwoods road in western Kentucky. Bears might have been after him, or Indians. But they weren't. Bears were asleep for the winter, and few Indians were seen in Kentucky any more. Indians were even scarcer than babies, and babies, thereabouts, were mighty scarce, or so it seemed to Dennis Hanks. That's why he was running so fast.

It was the 12th of February. And his cousin, Nancy Hanks Lincoln, had just had a baby boy. Tom Lincoln had come in town to tell of it, and to fetch Aunt Betsy Sparrow, who'd made a shirt and a "yaller" petticoat for the little fellow to wear. Tom and Nancy already had a girl named Sarah, who was two years old. But this baby was a baby BOY! Hearing that, nine-year-old Dennis had grabbed up his cap and set out on a run for the Lincolns' cabin. He had been running for two miles when he came at last to a clearing in the woods and he was there!

Before him, in the lonely clearing, stood a small, gray cabin, made of logs, with one door, one window and a big, mud-plastered chimney. From the chimney smoke was rising.

Inside, on a bed of saplings opposite the fireplace, Nancy was lying, her long, brown hair spread out on the corn-husk mattress, and the baby close beside her. She was half asleep when a banging on the door and a boy's voice broke into her dreams. There stood Dennis, puffing, and squinting about in the dim light.

"The baby?" he gasped." Where's he at? Cain't see 'im nowheres!"

Nancy smiled and beckoned to him, gently lifting a corner of the homespun blanket.

"Abraham," she said. "You've got a visitor. Abraham—that's what we figure to call him," she explained to Dennis in her soft slow drawl, "after his gran'pappy Linkern."

The boy took one look and the eager light faded from his face. Was this a baby? This little thing all red and wrinkly like a dried-up apple? All he could say was,

"He won't come to much, I reckon."

Nancy Lincoln did not answer. She had closed her eyes and slipped back again into the happier hopes and dreams that filled her heart that February morning.

Little Abe grew faster than a punkin' vine. Soon he could sit up and play with Sarah's corn-cob doll, and reach for the dog's tail. Next he was toddling about the cabin on legs so long and spindly they made his father laugh and reckon he'd soon be big enough "to tote a gun and go huntin' coons."

Hunting was Tom Lincoln's favorite occupation. Before they moved out to this half cleared farm, Tom and Nancy had lived in town. Tom had been a carpenter, and a handy one. But he'd rather go hunting any day than work with carpenter tools or grub away on the farm. So the corn and squash and potatoes he planted didn't always grow the way they should.

"The land's no good," he said, "all stumps and stones and yaller clay. Thing for us to do is to sell out and move."

So when Abe was about three, the Lincolns moved to what his father thought would be an easier farm to work, over on Knob Creek, about fifteen miles away. That was the first home Abe remembered, for they lived there in Knob Creek valley until he was seven.

HIRT TAIL BOY"

THE CORN MILL IN KENTUCKY

One summer morning, Abe was asleep on his sack of cornhusks on the cabin floor. A thin streak of sunlight, slanting in through the logs, fell upon his tight closed eyelids. He blinked, rolled over and sat up. At that, a scrubby little hound jumped up, all a-wriggle, here and there, to cover him with kisses.

Abe took the dog in his lap, and felt of its crooked front leg. The leg had been badly broken when he had found the poor little creature lying deserted in the road, a few weeks before.

"Looks to be all right now," he said. "Reckon you can go along today, with me and my friend Austin to the mill." Abe yawned.

He stood up, and stretched his arms high above his head of rumpled black hair. He was a big boy for seven, and very tall. Sometimes he wished he were not so tall. Boys wouldn't tease him then and call him "High."

Anyway, nobody could call him "Shirt-tail boy" again, he thought, drawing on his new buckskin breeches. Now he had pants to wear, too, like all big boys had; not just a little old dangly shirt.

Hodgen's Mill, where the Lincolns took their corn to be ground, was eight miles away. To get an early start, Abe had fetched in firewood the night before. Now he had only to feed his baby pig and his billy-goat, and get water from the spring. By the time he was back with his brimming buckets, Sarah was up. And his mother had corn meal cooking and salt pork sizzling in a long-handled frying pan.

Their father wasn't with them. He had gone off hunting. Not for game, this time, but for new land. Tom Lincoln had grown restless again and wanted to find a better place than Knob Creek for his family to live. But they didn't want a better place to live. This was home to them, this little valley settlement, with its corn-husking parties and its quilting bees.

Abe especially loved going to the mill. Lucky he was big enough now to go alone, he thought, lifting a sack of corn over one shoulder on the end of a stick. His mother stood in the door as he went off down the path, the little hound trotting at his heels. To her he didn't look so big. She wondered how he could carry that load of corn so far.

Austin was waiting for him, a piece up the road. He had his own sack of corn, and also a gun to protect them. There was a long, lonely stretch of road through the deep woods and he was afraid of meeting wolves, or even wildcats. "Ain't you, Abe?" he asked.

Abe shook his head. "Nope, not too much," he said and trudged along silently. He was thinking hard, and his lips were moving. Then he said suddenly; "T-R-KE. Turkey! Mebbe that's the way to spell it."

Austin didn't know and he didn't care. Abe understood. Some folks were like that. His own pappy. He'd say there was more use knowing how to shoot turkey than to spell it.

But not his mammy. She could read and write a little. In spring, when a teacher kept school in the settlement, she'd made their pappy let both him and Sarah go. And she'd say:

"Abe, you larn all you kin, and git to be of some account."

He couldn't get to school much because his

mammy took sick and he stayed with her. But he wanted to learn, as she said, and be of some account. Be a miller, like Mr. Hodgen, maybe, who had a town named after him! Mrs. Hodgen was teaching Abe to spell and count. She read to him, too, out of a wonderful book called *Aesop's Fables*. Abe had just finished telling Austin one of the fables as they got to the mill.

As usual, the dooryard was crowded. Men and boys stood about waiting their turn to have their corn ground into meal. A yoke of oxen went slowly round and round, turning the big grindstones. Abe and Austin had just passed by a gang of big boys, up to no good, when they heard a sharp yelp. Abe whirled about.

"Who hit my dog?" he said fiercely. "YOU?"

A fat, freckled boy grinned and nodded.

"Give 'im a punch. Fight 'im," said Austin.

Abe shook his head. Said he didn't want to fight unless he had to. The other boys hollered that he didn't dare to.

Just then Mr. Hodgen appeared on the scene and settled the argument. Each boy, he said, was to lift the other by the seat of the pants and shake him hard. Abe tried first, and did it, and then stooped over. Freckles grabbed hold, but couldn't even raise Abe off the ground.

So he guessed he'd not throw stones again at Abe's "little ole houn' dawg."

Austin went home that day, prouder than ever to be the friendliest friend of Abe Linkern, the smartest, strongest boy he knew. But queer, too, kind of mournful. Now as they walked home, Abe looked as if he didn't have a friend in the world. Austin tried talking about their favorite plan of running the mill together when they grew up. But Abe just shook his head and looked even sadder. Maybe he'd never even go to the mill again, he said.

Any day, now, his father might be coming back. Then he'd take them away to live—to a far-off, lonesome place, called Indianny!

Abe couldn't talk about it. All he could do was to try to swallow the lump in his throat and hold back the tears till he got home. Then he lay down in his corner of the cabin with the little dog beside him, and sobbed himself to sleep. Inside, he wasn't a very big boy. He was only seven.

INDIANA

Summer days went by, and autumn with its falling leaves. Then came one gray-brown evening in November—the last one before they left for Indiana. Dusk was folding about the little cabin as Abe came slowly trailing in from saying good-bye to Austin, and leaving him his pet crow. Through the open door he saw the firelight on his mammy's face, and heard her soft voice saying Bible words: "The Lord is my shepherd, I shall not want." He stood there listening. "Yea," she was saying, "though I walk through the valley of the shadow of death, I shall fear no evil."

He went in quietly and sat down on the low bench close behind her, until she had finished the last words.

"They comfort me," she said.

Abe nodded. He felt better too. The strange, beautiful words seemed to reach way down inside, to the part of him that hurt.

By sunrise next morning, two scrawny old horses stood outside the cabin door. His mother and Sarah were busy folding up the blankets and

BACK

OODS

packing in the pewter plates. His father whistled and sang as he picked up the iron kettle and frying pan, and handed Abe a few other things to carry out.

"The furniture's wuthless," he said. "Not near good enough fur my sweet purty Nancy and her fine new cabin in Indianny."

Nancy smiled and wondered if there'd be a travelling preacher to come around, same as here in Kentucky, so they could hear him read the Bible. Tom was sure of it. "Everything'd be jes' the way they wanted it, once they got to Pigeon Creek in Indianny."

Dennis Hanks wished he were going with them, when they stopped in Elizabethtown to say goodbye to Uncle Tom and Aunt Betsy Sparrow. Next year, Aunt Betsy said, they might be moving over, too. They'd a hankering to cross the Ohio River. Folks said the Ohio was the biggest, broadest river you could ever imagine.

Next day, Abe thought so, too, when they came to it and were crossing the wide, shining water in a ferryboat.

The Ohio River separated Kentucky from Indiana. And it did more than that, his father said. It separated all the states where rich folks could own slaves from states where the law said they couldn't. That was why it was good for poor folks like them to be going over.

From the river, there were sixteen miles more to go, back into the deep woods. Deeper and thicker woods than any in Kentucky. In places there wasn't even a trail. Abe's father had borrowed a wagon to carry in supplies for the winter, and he often had to chop down trees in order to get through. And when they got there, there was nothing to be seen.

Just a pile of brush and some notched trees to mark the spot.

First thing to do, his father said, was to make a pole shed to live in, till they could get a cabin built. Abe helped. They cut down saplings and stood them up into a three-sided shed, open in the front.

There, in that open shed, they spent the long winter. The cold rain and snow blew in upon them, and sometimes smoke from the log fire outside. They cooked their meals of game and wild turkey over the fire, and kept it burning all night to scare away the wolves, howling in the darkness.

One bright day, Abe's father marked out on the ground the space for the new cabin. It was to be a big one, with a loft to sleep in and pegs in the wall to climb up to it. Short, cold days were spent chopping down the trees and hewing the logs. Spring came and summer. The walls were up, the chimney built and the roof on. They moved in.

Then Uncle Tom and Aunt Betsy Sparrow came and lived in the old pole shed. But not for long. They both died, the second summer, of a strange, incurable illness.

Nancy nursed and cared for them, and then caught the fever herself.

About a mile from the cabin was a spring, and a soft, sandy spot where the deer came down to drink, with their little spotted fawns. All about were the deep, quiet woods, warm and sweet-smelling and filled with a shimmering green light. It was there in that quiet spot, that, later, they buried Nancy Lincoln.

She did not live to see the "fine new cabin" finished or the furniture made. Tom meant to do it and to clear more fields and get the farm started better. But there were too many good days to go hunting! So the cabin had no window at all, no door—just a hole cut out—and no floor laid over the black earth. And when she lay ill and burning up with the strange fever, Nancy lay as always, on a bed of poles and a mattress filled with cornhusks.

Abe ran with cool cups of water, but each day she grew worse. At last she held his hand and told him to be good to Sarah and his pappy. And to believe that God knows what is best. And then —she never spoke again.

Abe was nine. With tears streaming down his face, he helped his father build his mother's coffin. As he followed it slowly through the woodsy path, he kept thinking of the words she used to say about walking through the valley of death and fearing no evil. If only there could be a preacher to read from the Bible over her grave! That's what she would have wanted, he knew. But travelling preachers were seldom seen in those deep, dark woods of Indiana.

HIS GOOD STEPMOTHER

A whole year passed in misery and loneliness. Then Abe's father couldn't stand it any longer. He went back to Kentucky, leaving Abe and Sarah alone with Dennis Hanks. Dennis had come to live in their cabin after Aunt Betsy died.

One dismal December day, Abe sat by the fire, scratching all the letters he could remember in the ashes, wishing he knew how to read. Every day seemed like a week, waiting for his father to come back. Abe knew why he'd gone, but that didn't make waiting any easier. Dennis had just come in with his gun, bringing a squirrel for dinner. Sarah said she'd cook it and try to make it taste good. Abe said he couldn't eat. He couldn't even swallow.

What if nobody would come? he thought. Or what if somebody came, and she didn't like them —him and Sarah? What if. . . . All of a sudden he heard horses' hooves. He ran outside. And, almost before he knew it, SHE was there. His stepmother, Sarah Bush Lincoln. He saw her first, sitting beside his father on the seat of a big wagon, piled so high with furniture that it took four horses to pull it.

On top of the pile sat two girls and a boy. They jumped down as the wagon stopped and stood staring at Abe and Sarah in their dirty, ragged clothes. Then the tall, straight woman came and stood beside them.

"These are my children," she said. "John and Sarah and Matilda Johnston." Her voice was warm and friendly. "And I suppose you are Sarah Lincoln? And you," she added slowly, "you must be Abraham."

Abe looked up. Her eyes were as friendly as her voice. She didn't even seem to see that he was too tall, or mind that he was homely. She just smiled, and so Abe smiled, too. From then to the end of his life, this second mother was to be "the best friend he had."

"Wa-al now," she said briskly, stepping into the cabin. "Fust thing for me to do is to make something for us all to eat. Meantime you young-uns go out to the horse trough. Take this soft soap and wash up good, all over."

Wash up? thought Abe, all over? in the winter?

That was a mighty queer notion. But he did it, and it felt good. It felt good, too, to have a comb run through his gritty black hair. And to put on a clean shirt of the Johnston boy's. And sit down to good, hot food with eight folks around the table to eat it.

After supper, his new mother swept up the dirty cabin. But to be halfway decent, she told Abe's father, it would have to have a wood floor and a door and windows. Then he could get some lime over to Gentryville and whitewash the walls. Right away, that night, everybody must help carry in the furniture and unroll the feather beds. Abe heard something bumping in the chest as they set it down.

Next morning, when his stepmother opened it, there were two books. One was the Bible. And the other—he could hardly believe his eyes—the other was his beloved fable book.

It was *Aesop's Fables*.

"Kin you read?" his stepmother asked. Abe shook his head. "Nor kin I," she added quickly. "But you'd like to learn?" She knew the answer before he gave it. "Then I'll make sure that you

THE FAMILY

git the chance, soon as there's enough settlers around here to have a school start up."

The winter Abe was thirteen, a school was started. All the children went for a few months. The others didn't half try, but Abe was different. He went over and over the words in the Speller, and practiced writing everywhere, specially on the back of the big, wooden fire shovel.

Dennis got interested, and made a pen for him out of a turkey buzzard's quill, stirred up some ink, and brought back some paper from the store at Gentryville to make into a notebook. In it Abe wrote:

Abraham Lincoln
his hand and pen.
he will be good but
god knows When

He was now fourteen. At last he could read and write! All day long, his father had chores for him to do—hard, grubby work—but as soon as he could lay down his axe and hoe, he was turning the pages of a book, reading as if he were starved.

Tom Lincoln couldn't understand it. "It'd be different," he'd say, "if he was puny or sickly, so's he couldn't go huntin'. But for a big strappin' feller like Abe to take so to book-larnin' is jes' plain queer."

But the good stepmother understood this boy who was so different from the others. Sometimes, as she was patching or knitting, he'd have her listen while he read a funny story aloud, and they'd laugh over it together.

The first book Abe ever owned, he got from the first man he ever worked for, Mr. Josiah Crawford, a nearby farmer.

Mr. Crawford was a thin, sour man, with such a way of hanging onto money that he had more of it than any of his neighbors, and could hire them to work for him.

Tom Lincoln helped build him a new farmhouse and then sent young Abe over to work as a hired man. Abe was then only fifteen, but close to six feet tall, and strong as he was tall.

One day, Mr. Crawford and two or three other

men were puzzling over how to lift a heavy log chicken coop that he wanted moved.

"Whar's Abe?" he cried in his thin, sour voice. "Off readin' again?"

"Mebbe," said one of the men, "or mebbe down by the road, talking to a stranger. You know Abe—cain't let a traveler get by without findin' out all he knows."

Just then the big boy sauntered up.

"Movin' the coop?" he drawled. "Whar to?"

The men pointed. Abe stooped down, hoisted it onto his back, carried it over and set it down, all by himself. The men were dumfounded.

Oh, Abe was strong, no doubt of that, agreed his employer, but he was lazy. He could husk corn, chop down trees, split rails faster than any two men, if he took a notion, but he'd rather read than work.

Josiah, himself didn't care much about books, but he owned a few. He let Abe take one home, warning him to be careful of it. It was a biography of George Washington.

Abe could hardly wait to start it, and then he couldn't bear to stop. He read all evening, stretched out by the fire, until his father banked it with ashes and made him go to bed. Abe slept in the loft. To have the book handy as soon as it grew light, he carried it up with him, and laid it carefully between the logs. Next morning when he reached for it, his heart sank. It was soaking wet. There had been rain in the night. What could he do or say?

"Wa-al," said Josiah Crawford, shrewdly. "Seein' it's you Abe . . . You put in three days huskin' corn, and you kin keep it."

Only three days! Abe could hardly believe it. When those three days were over the book belonged to him. The story of George Washington's life. He read it again and again. Each time it stirred him with ambition.

"I'm not always going' to grub and shuck corn and split rails for a livin'," he said to Mrs. Crawford, one morning. And when she asked him what he wanted to do or be, he answered,

"The President." He half smiled as if he were joking, but his voice was serious. "Well, anyway, I'll study and get ready," he said, "and the chance may come."

THE RIVER AND THE LAW

From daybreak to dark, Abe worked as a hired farm hand, until he was past seventeen. For a while he lived with a farmer near the Ohio River who paid him six dollars a month. The most he ever earned was 30 cents a day for butchering hogs, until that wonderful, never-to-be-forgotten day out on the Ohio River.

He had built a flatboat, and was standing on it, out in the middle of the river, looking up at a high, white, whistling steamboat, with a paddle wheel and a smoking funnel. Down from the deck, flying toward him over the water, came two silver half-dollars. He caught them. There they lay in his hand, bright as bits of the river itself!

One dollar!

He had earned one whole dollar. And with so little work. He had been on shore, tinkering with his boat, when two strangers had driven up. They had wanted to catch a steamboat going down the river. Steamboats couldn't come in close to shore, so Abe had ferried them out and carried their trunks on board.

And for just that, they had thrown him a dollar! From now on, why shouldn't he work on the river? If he could get a boatload of stuff to sell, why couldn't he take it down the Mississippi River to New Orleans? Every day, flatboats were going by, loaded with pork, turkeys, corn meal, potatoes—all kinds of stuff that farmers were sending down the river to be sold. Why shouldn't he do it, too?

Why? said his father. Because he was too young. And because they never could get enough off their poor farm to have anything to sell.

So Abe had to wait. Still he kept quizzing the old rivermen, finding out how to go about it if his chance ever came.

Meanwhile, he got a part-time job over at Jones's store, in Gentryville, and also ran his ferryboat, out from the Indiana shore.

One day two Kentucky fellows who ran a ferry out from their side of the river had him arrested and taken before a Kentucky judge.

"This here Indianny feller's got no right," they said, "to be runnin' passengers across the river. It's agin' the law."

The judge asked Abe if he ever took them beyond the middle of the river. No? Then, said the judge, he was not breaking the law.

The LAW! thought Abe. Here was something else he ought to find out about. After that, he went over, as often as he could, to listen in the courtroom of the Kentucky judge.

And, from an Indiana judge, he borrowed a book to read about the laws of Indiana. Some were exactly opposite to the laws of Kentucky, like the one about owning slaves.

There were United States laws, too, for all of the states together. In his book Abe found the first United States laws ever made. They were called the CONSTITUTION. On another page was the DECLARATION OF INDEPENDENCE. This told why the states had wanted to unite in the first place and form a new nation.

All this was hard to understand, Abe thought, but mighty interesting to puzzle over. The words, "All men are created equal." Just what did those words mean? he wondered.

Whatever he read he kept turning over in his mind, until he could say it in his own words.

Down at Jones's store, he soon noticed, whenever he got to telling about what he'd read in the law-book, and trying to make it clear with a funny story or two, the crowd would all gather around to listen.

The year that Andrew Jackson was elected President, it seemed as if every farmer around Gentryville was worked up about the law. To think that Andrew Jackson, just a poor, plain man like themselves, could work up to the highest office in the land! Didn't that prove what the law said—that everybody in this country had a free and equal chance?

1828, the year Andrew Jackson was elected, Abe was nineteen, and made his first trip down the Mississippi River to New Orleans. Mr. Gentry of Gentryville, a rich farmer, hired him to go with his son Allen. The boys built a big flat-boat; loaded it with farm products to sell. And in early spring, with Abe at the forward oar, they pushed boldly out into the current and were off.

It was a journey of 1000 miles from the wooded shores of Indiana to the steamy bayous and swamps of the lower Mississippi. And a great adventure. Traveling by day, watching out for snags and sandbars, and tying up at the shore by night.

One dark night, down among the sugar plantations, they were almost asleep, when they heard footsteps on the deck. They jumped up. A gang of Negro slaves had come aboard to steal.

"Get a gun, Abe!" shouted his partner.

He was sure that the slaves would fight to kill rather than be caught. Abe grabbed a club, and drove them off the boat. But he came back with a gash in his forehead and blood streaming in his eyes. No more sleep that night. They cut loose and floated down the river. A day or so later, they were pulling into a wharf piled high with cotton bales.

They were in New Orleans! Soon they were walking its narrow streets, peering into flowery courtyards, and up at lacy iron balconies. And they were listening to the strange talk of foreign sailors, whose ships, flying flags from every nation in the world, were anchored in that harbor. Wonderful sights there were in the fascinating old city for those two boys from the backwoods of Indiana to see and think about.

And evil ones, too. For this old city of New Orleans was one of the great slave markets of the south. All about him on the walls, Abe could see advertisements posted, offering to buy or sell for cash "good likely negroes," male or female, house servants or field hands.

In the market place, he saw them paraded up and down on the auction block, so that the buyers might see what they were about to bid on. They were sold just like horses or mules, back in Indiana. It was horrible to see.

Even so, as Abe knew, it was lawful. The United States law said that people south of the Ohio River could own slaves. And if it was lawful to own them, it was lawful to buy and sell them. It couldn't be done away with, he supposed, except by changing the law.

A flatboat was good only for floating down stream. So the boys went back up the Mississippi on one of those high, white river steamboats with the smoking funnels. Abe was home by June. His father, he found, was then beginning to talk about moving again.

LAKE MICHIGAN
CHICAGO
INDIANA
HIS WAS
SPRINGFIE
NEW SALEM
HOME
FATHER'S FARM
PIGEON CREEK
SANGAMON RIVER
SANGAMON COUNTY
THE WAY THEY CAME
VANDALIA
BLACK HAWK VILLAGE
ILLINOIS
MISSISSIPPI

1830

February 12, 1830, Abraham Lincoln was 21 years old. Three days after his birthday, he was moving with the family to Illinois.

For seven years he had lived where he was born, in the hills of Kentucky. Fourteen more, in the forests of Indiana. Now for a good part of his life, the great prairie state of Illinois was to be his home.

The wagon, which he had made to carry the family and their belongings, had stood for several days before the cabin door. It was a huge covered wagon, with big wooden wheels, sliced from the trunk of a tree, and drawn by a yoke of red-brown oxen.

It was none too big. They even needed another wagon. For thirteen people, Hankses, Lincolns, Johnstons, all of them were going. All except Sarah, Abe's sister, who had died soon after she was married. All of the young folks were now married, except Abe. Mathilda Johnston was Mrs. Dennis Hanks.

"Aunt Sairey" (Abe's stepmother), as Dennis told it, took charge of getting the whole unwieldy tribe packed up and started.

Abe, he said, kept them cheered up along the way, telling yarns and jokes as he walked beside the oxen, cracking his whip. Whenever they got bogged down in the half frozen mud, he schemed up some way to get them out of it, and looked after everything. One poor little dog got left behind, crossing a stream. Abe couldn't bear to see it shivering and shaking, and waded back after it.

It was John Hanks, another cousin of Abe's, who had urged his relatives to come to Illinois. He had sent back word of the rich black soil, of the level prairie land, of the wild grass that grew higher than a man. Game was still plentiful, he said, and farming was easy. No forests there to be cut down. No sandy hills to plow. Only here and there, rich groves of trees and bluffs along the rivers.

One river and county were called the SANGAMON, which was an Indian name meaning "land of plenty to eat."

"Land of plenty to eat." That sounded so good to Tom Lincoln! He was willing to sell his old Indiana farm for less than he paid for it, just to be on his way to that happy land.

After one winter there, when the snow lay seven feet deep, the newcomers decided it was too cold for them in Sangamon County. So they moved south a hundred miles or so, to Goose Nest Prairie. There Abe helped his father build another cabin.

There he split rails again, and laid them out into long zigzag fences.

Those long, crooked fence rails. Years later they were to mark another great change in his life, as they did now.

For now, having split them, Abraham Lincoln laid down his axe, said goodbye and left home to make his own way in the world. Until he was of age, his work and all that he earned had belonged to his father. But no longer. Now he was past 21. He was free to go and do with his life whatever he would or could.

He was strong. He knew how to work. He could read and write and figure a little. That was all. Still he could hope and dream and try to amount to something.

And he could know, as he put his arms around his good stepmother and she held him close, that "the best friend he had in the world" would always believe in him.

NEW SALEM

On a high ridge overlooking the Sangamon River was a little string of log cabins forming the village of New Salem. Trudging up the road from the river, one day in that summer of 1831, came tall, awkward Abraham Lincoln, carrying a small bundle. He had come to live in New Salem, Illinois. And he was arriving, by chance, on the best of all days to become acquainted. Men of the village were holding an election, and had just discovered that they needed another clerk. At that moment tall, awkward Abe sauntered down the street, casting a long shadow in the sun.

"Howdy, stranger," said a short man squinting up at him. "Mebbe you kin help us out. By any chance, kin you write?"

Abe grinned. "Reckon I kin make a few rabbit tracks," he said. So he sat down. All day he recorded the names of the voters and stored them up in his memory. Whenever business grew slack, he tipped his chair back against the wall and told of comical things he'd seen or heard of back in Indianny. Everybody took a fancy to him.

Abe had come to clerk for a man named Offutt in his new grocery store, which, however, wasn't yet built. So, before long, he was out with his axe, chopping down logs and building it. And Offutt was boasting about having hired such a smart young fellow.

"That Abe Lincoln," he said, "knows more'n any man I ever saw. And I bet he can beat any man in Sangamon County in a wrestling match."

"Is tha-a-a-t so?" sneered Bill Clary, who kept a store next door, specializing in whiskey. "I'd jes' like to see him wrestle Jack Armstrong—he'd have a tough time there."

"Yeah, jes' let 'im try it," said another one of the rough, tough Clary Grove gang. They didn't think much of Abe because he never drank.

The match was arranged. Abe said he didn't like such "mauling and pulling," but he knew he had to prove what he could do. A crowd came from miles around. Jack Armstrong was stocky and solid as a bull. But Abe was tough as old hickory, and his arms were longer. Jack was held off at arm's length, till he lost his temper and ground the heel of his boot onto Abe's instep. The next thing he knew he was flat on his back. When he got to his feet, he saw his gang swarming toward Lincoln with their fists up.

"Lay off, boys," cried their former champion, pushing through the crowd. "Abe Lincoln fights fair. Shake hands with him. He's the best feller ever broke into this here settlement."

In the store, as soon as he had it built, Abe kept on making friends. Customers soon saw that he was absolutely honest. Whatever they bought, coffee or calico, salt or sugar, cheese, tea or molasses, he gave them full measure.

One day, by mistake, he let one woman go home with not enough tea. So he wrapped up a quarter of a pound and walked four miles out to Clary's Grove to take it to her. Back in town when they laughed at him, he chuckled and said that he reckoned he didn't do so bad, at that. She'd invited him to a fine hot supper. Othewise he'd had to pay all of nineteen cents for his meal at the Rutledge Tavern.

But, he thought to himself, he would have

NEW SALEM
TAVERN

seen Ann. Ann Rutledge, with her blue, blue eyes and her coppery gold hair. Just to have her look at him made Abe's heart beat faster and his ears grow hot. But he had to laugh. What would such a pretty girl ever see in him—a poor homely scrub from the backwoods?

And yet her father, he knew, had spoken well of him. After hearing him speak at the new Debating Society, Mr. Rutledge had said:

"That young man speaks well. All he lacks is culture to reach a high place in life."

Abe's friend the schoolmaster, said that to speak better one needed to study grammar. Abe walked six miles to borrow a grammar book and then studied grammar hour after hour, all winter, until he had mastered the rules.

By spring, he had made so many friends, and they were so encouraging, that he made up his mind to try his luck at politics. He wanted to represent Sangamon County in the Illinois State Legislature. When election time came, his friends in and around New Salem voted for him. But not enough people in the rest of the county knew him, so he was defeated.

Just before that happened, something else came along—the Black Hawk War. Black Hawk, a great Indian chief, had led his braves back across the Mississippi River into their old homeland of Illinois. The governor called for volunteers to drive them out again. Jack Armstrong and the Clary Grove boys enlisted in the company formed in New Salem. And to Abe's great satisfaction, they choose him to be their captain. CAPTAIN Abraham Lincoln!

What did he know about military rules and regulations? Precious little, outside of "FORWARD MARCH!" and "HALT!" But he had quick wits and he knew how to use them.

He marched off to war in northern Illinois and up into Wisconsin, and didn't halt until Black Hawk was defeated. Then he came home again, having killed plenty of mosquitoes, he said, but not a single Indian.

Meanwhile, Offutt's store had gone completely to pieces. And Abe was out of a job.

"Why not be a blacksmith?" someone suggested. Abe shook his head. Pounding on an anvil all day would give him no time to read. In the army he had met a Major Stuart, a lawyer, who had talked to him about the law. That was what he wanted to read about now, as soon as he found where he could borrow the right books.

Keeping store would give him time to read, between customers. So he decided to open up a store with a young man named Berry. They borrowed $1000 to buy their stock, expecting to pay it back when the firm of BERRY & LINCOLN began making money. It never did. Berry paid too much attention to the whiskey barrel. And Abe spent his time reading Shakespeare, studying the law and visiting with people who came in for their mail. For then, in 1833, he was also Postmaster of New Salem. It was not a big job, but he liked it, because it gave him the right to read any newspapers that came, and so learn all the excitement going on in Washington. The lawbooks he found, by chance, in a barrel of old stuff which he had bought for fifty cents one day merely to accommodate a stranger.

The poor store, with so little attention paid to it, just naturally "winked out." Berry died of drink. And Lincoln was left with the whole debt of $1000. Worse off than he had ever been, he had to go back to splitting rails and doing odd jobs for a living.

At the same time, a young man named McNamar was making money in the store right next door, and was engaged to marry Ann Rutledge.

Poor Abe was so sunk in gloom that he went to bed at night dreading to see the sun rise on another day. Would he always be a failure? Would he never be of any account?

One day he was out working with his axe, wondering if he'd ever have a chance to try again, when he saw a friend coming his way.

"Know anything about surveying, Abe?" he asked. The Chief Surveyor of Sangamon County, he said, was in need of a helper. Thousands of people were now coming into Illinois. Acres of prairie land had to be measured off, new towns laid out, and miles of new wagon roads.

Abe's face lighted up. Not that he knew anything about surveying. But did that stop him from learning? No. Nothing ever had, or ever would stop Abraham Lincoln from learning.

First he walked to Springfield, twenty miles

away, to talk to the surveyor and to get a book on surveying. Next he got his friend, the schoolmaster, to help him with the mathematics. Then he studied hour after hour, night after night, until he grew so thin and hollow-eyed that all of his friends were worried about him.

"Lay off for a day," urged Squire Bowling Green, "come out to our place and rest."

Abe wouldn't stop. And in the amazingly short time of six weeks he was ready to start out with his surveying instruments.

Jack Armstrong went as his helper. Before they set out, Hannah, Jack's wife, put leather patches on Abe's pants. While she sewed he held the baby, "Duff" or rocked him in his cradle.

All over Sangamon County Abe traveled, laying out roads and streets, setting up markers. He made many good and lasting friends, who were never to forget his comical ways or his kindly heart.

In the fall, all those new friends voted for him as their Representative from Sangamon County to the State Legislature. And he was elected. It was 1834 when he went off to the state capital at Vandalia for his first term.

And after that first term, when he returned to New Salem in the spring, he was engaged to marry his beautiful Ann Rutledge.

No one knew where McNamar was. He had disappeared. Many months ago, he had kissed Ann goodbye and left on the stagecoach for the east, promising to be back soon, so that they could be married. But he had never come back nor even written.

And so when Ann looked up at faithful, kindly Abe, she saw in him what she had not seen before, and gave her love for his. He had never been so happy as he was in those summer evenings, planning their future.

Then, in August, Ann died. It was almost more than Abe could bear. He flung himself on her grave and sobbed. He walked alone at night and up and down the river in the autumn rain. He would talk to no one. Finally he went to stay a while with Squire Bowling Green and Nancy and they helped him to look forward again.

Winter came, and he was back in his seat in the State Legislature, and very busy. He was scheming up a way to get the State capital moved to Springfield, in Sangamon County. He also met Major Stuart again, who encouraged him to keep on studying to become a lawyer. So the next summer, Abe was walking back and forth to Stuart's law office in Springfield to borrow law books, one after another. Months of studying went by; he finally passed his test and had the right to sign himself:

A. Lincoln Esq
Atty & Counsellor at Law

In the spring of 1837, just six years after he had come up the road from the river with his bundle, Abraham Lincoln left New Salem for Springfield, to become a partner in the new law firm of STUART & LINCOLN.

But he was still dismally poor. As he rode off on a borrowed horse, the old debt trailed behind him like a long black shadow. All his possessions were in the two saddlebags. And when he got to Springfield, he had hardly enough money to rent a room. He felt mighty lucky when young Joshua Speed let him share the room above his store.

MARY TODD

Springfield was the perfect place for little Miss Mary Todd to look for the kind of husband she had set her heart upon. It had just been made the new capital of Illinois and was full of young politicians, Democrats and Whigs.

Mary Todd was eighteen, little and pretty and smart, and knew exactly what she wanted. She had just arrived in 1839 from Lexington, Kentucky, where her father, Robert Todd, was president of the bank. But, said Mary:

"The man I marry is going to be President of the United States."

That was what she told the girls at school. That was what she had told her sister Elizabeth even before she had unpacked her bags or untied the strings of her taffeta bonnet. At the very moment, almost, that the little lady had stepped from the stagecoach, she had announced her ambition.

Mary had come to live in Springfield with her sister and brother-in-law, Mr. and Mrs. Ninian Edwards, who had the finest house in town. It was of red brick and had a wide porch running around it, and tall windows with long swooped-up curtains and carpets with red roses on them. It was very elegant for Springfield, but not good enough for Mary.

The only house that Mary wanted to live in was the White House in Washington. She was dreaming about it, and about the gorgeous gowns she would wear, as she stood at one of the long upstairs windows, on a winter afternoon, pinning a pink rose in her hair.

She was also watching a young man coming up the brick walk to call upon her. He was very, very short, and very small, but it was plain to see from the way he walked that he felt himself to be as big and powerful as a giant.

He was Stephen A. Douglas, a most promising young Democrat.

Mary had met and waltzed with Mr. Douglas at a big Ball, early in the season. She had singled him out as one of the two young politicians most likely to succeed.

The other one, Mr. Abraham Lincoln, a Whig, could hardly dance at all. But he had a strange way with him, and every time he came to call, she liked him better.

"But you have no idea of ever marrying him, I hope," said her sister, one afternoon at dinner. "He's not suitable for you at all."

"Don't consider him, Mary," said her brother-in-law. "He comes, you know, from poor, shiftless white trash that can't even read or write."

Mary's eyes flashed. Nobody need tell her what to do! Abraham Lincoln was coming to call that very night, she said, and she had made up her mind to marry him. "Because," she added, "I think he will be President, some day."

With that, she flounced out of the room and upstairs, to pin a whole wreath of pink roses in her smooth brown hair.

At the same time, upstairs in the low room above the store of his friend Josh Speed, Abraham Lincoln was "sprucing up" for the call. He was blacking his boots, brushing his black hair, and squinting at his face in a wiggly mirror, as he put on his brand new, high, black, stovepipe hat.

"Powerful homely feller to go callin' on a

SPRINGF
HALL
GROCERIES
HARDWARE
BOOTS
SHOES
CLO
CRO

DAILY INDEPENDENT
PRINTING
DENTAL ROOMS
DRUGS

purty little lady," he said, but he went.

Soon he was at the red brick house sitting opposite Miss Mary in the parlor and fascinated by her. She was so sparkly and shiny-like! He leaned forward, and just watched her while she talked about everything—French, Geometry, Politics. Almost before he knew it, they were sitting close together on the rosewood sofa, engaged to be married.

Then he was worried. How could he ever make her happy? Poor as he was, he couldn't! Night and day he worried and brooded. He tried to tell her she was making a mistake.

She wept and wouldn't listen to him. He was utterly wretched. They didn't see each other for many months.

Then suddenly, all in a hurry, one November morning, they decided to be married, got the preacher, invited a few friends and were married that very evening by lamplight in the parlor of the Edwards' house.

November 4, 1842, it was, that Miss Mary Todd became the wife of Abraham Lincoln, but she had eighteen years to wait before she could know that the man she had chosen was going to be President. Luck seemed to desert him all of those long dreary years, while the sunlight of success shone on Stephen A. Douglas.

The very next year, in 1843, that confident young Democrat was elected to the House of Representatives, and went gaily off to Congress and the nation's capital.

That year, Mary and Abraham were still living in one room in the Globe Tavern, and Bobbie was born. He was named for his grandfather Todd—Robert Todd Lincoln.

The next year, they had saved just enough money to buy a small white house on the edge of town. Mary cleaned and cooked, and took care of the baby boys (for soon there were two of them). She made her own clothes, and tried to make her untidy husband keep on his coat and necktie, and got so discouraged and worn out sometimes she was ready to shriek. Lincoln fed the horse, milked the cow, shoveled snow, cut grass, chopped wood, tended to his law business and tried to be patient with Mary.

At last, 1846, he was elected a Representative

to Congress. But that year, Stephen A. Douglas was made a Senator, still pacing out ahead of Abe, like a little giant.

Lincoln went to Washington, hoping to make a good record that would please the Whigs of Illinois who had elected him. Instead, he made a speech that made them furious. He said that the war, which then (in 1848) was going on between the United States and Mexico, was wrong. He honestly believed it. But for that, they called him dreadful names, even a traitor.

So he came home, at the end of his term, set down his carpet bag in the hall of the little house, hung his high, black hat on the hall tree, with a heavy heart.

His career in politics was over and done for, he believed. He said so to Mrs. Lincoln.

"Unless," he added, "you'd like to go out to Oregon. I might be made the governor."

"Oregon!" shrieked Mary, in a sharp, high voice. "Isn't Springfield dead enough? Why should we go and bury ourselves in Oregon?"

"All right, Molly, all right," he said patiently, "I only suggested it. We'll stay here."

LAWYER

The summer sun was hot next morning, as Abraham Lincoln walked toward his office. A dry prairie wind was blowing dust in circles across the town square and the courthouse steps. The swinging sign, with gold letters, saying

LINCOLN & HERNDON

creaked in the wind as he passed under it and climbed a flight of wooden steps. At the end of a narrow hall, he stopped for a moment and then turned a wobbly knob. The door opened on a drab room, lighted by a dirty window. Piles of newspapers in wild disorder lay upon a table.

A young man sat reading one of them. He glanced up, then jumped to his feet. It was young William Herndon, Lincoln's partner.

"Lincoln," he cried: "Mr. Lincoln! You're back! You're here!"

"Yes, I'm here, Billy," said the older man. But he'd been thinking it seemed hardly fair to start in just where they left off, when Billy had been home doing all the work.

Billy saw it otherwise. Hadn't Mr. Lincoln helped him to become a lawyer? Could he ever forget how grateful he had been when Mr. Lincoln had asked him to become his partner? Or how proud, when he had first seen his name shining in gold letters on that sign?

Such warm loyalty was irresistible. A slow smile crept over Lincoln's sad face. With a deep sigh, he removed his high black hat, set it on the table upside down and dropped a letter into it. Tucked inside of it, as usual, were several other envelopes and scraps of paper, for safekeeping.

Next he slipped off his long linen coat, unwound his necktie, and made himself comfortable in a wooden armchair tilted far back against the wall.

Then he was ready to tell of what he had done and seen in the east and answer Billy's many and various questions.

What was Washington like? And the Capitol building? Had he met Daniel Webster and Henry Clay? What did he think of Niagara Falls, and Boston, and Philadelphia? And of the new railroads that were now being built—had they replaced the stagecoach entirely in the east? And of the new land that the United States had just taken from Mexico—California and all of the great southwest. Would there be slavery in that new territory—or not? And above all—WHAT about the slave markets in Washington? Was there no way of getting rid of them? Or better still, getting rid of slavery entirely?

"Wipe it out. ABOLISH it. Get rid of it. That's what must be done," said Herndon earnestly. "The ABOLITIONISTS are absolutely right!"

"No," said Lincoln calmly. "I don't agree with you. Slavery is wrong. But I think that if we leave it alone where it is, it will die out gradually. What we must do is to keep it from spreading into any new territory."

He sat silent a moment, looking out of the window. Something they had said reminded him of a funny story which he told, and that reminded him of another one. Then he guessed it must be getting on toward dinner time. Mrs. Lincoln would be expecting him home. And he had promised the little boys to play with them.

So he'd best be moseying along. Tomorrow morning, he'd get back into the swing of things.

And, he added, tilting forward and bringing his feet down with a bang, GET TO BE A BETTER LAWYER!

"That's the main thing I've learned from going east. Those men in the east are better educated, better trained than we are. They can prove a point 'beyond the shadow of a doubt.' Those men will be coming out here, someday, and I'm going to be ready for them. I'm going to get a Geometry, and study it, and try to train my mind to think as clear and straight as they do."

He was about to sit down again, but the door burst open. There was Bobbie, who said that his mother said to come right straight home before the whole dinner was all dried up and spoilt.

The hot summer days passed finally, one by one, and September came.

One morning Bobbie and his little brother stood under the tree by the barn, each munching a big, yellow apple and watching while their father hitched up "Old Tom" to the one-seated buggy. Then he tossed in his well-worn carpet bag and faded umbrella, asked them for a big hug and a kiss, and started off on what he told them was called "riding the circuit."

Whatever that might mean, it sounded exciting to them. And so it was to their father.

Riding the circuit was the part of his law business that Abraham Lincoln liked best.

Out on the open prairie, under the wide sky there was time and space for a man to stretch his mind and soul.

"Riding the circuit" actually meant going about with fat, jolly Judge Davis, and other friendly lawyers in a circle of little towns, each one the head of a county in that part of Illinois. There was not enough to keep a lawyer busy in just one town or county seat. So, each spring and fall, the judge and lawyers traveled about, holding court and trying cases.

Evenings, they would gather in one of the little hotel rooms, enjoying one another's company and swapping stories half of the night.

Like a troup of traveling actors, they caused excitement wherever they arrived.

"Lincoln's come!" The word would pass among the townspeople. Lincoln was the favorite. The courtroom was always crowded when he was to speak. He could make the jury weep or roar with laughter. And he was a sight to see, pacing back and forth across the room, coat off, one thumb in the single suspender that held up his wrinkled trousers, talking as if the fate of his client hung on every word he said.

And he was full of surprises. At a critical moment, he would turn up with something unexpected, like the almanac in the case of "Duff" Armstrong.

"Duff" was the son of Lincoln's old friend Jack. He was the baby Abe had rocked in its cradle. Duff had been accused of murder and the evidence seemed all against him. His father was dead. But Hannah, his poor mother, was there in the courtroom, in her old sunbonnet, tense and anxious as each witness took the stand.

"I seen 'im when he done it," said one witness. "The moon was shining bright as day."

"You're sure about that?" asked Lincoln.

The witness was sure, positive, he swore to it.

Lincoln drew from his pocket a small paper almanac. He turned to the right month and showed that on that particular night there was NO moon! He appealed to the jury, won their sympathy and the boy was set free.

The founders of a new town were so fond of Lincoln that they told him one day that they wanted to name it after him.

"I'd be proud and honored," he said. "But," he added with an odd smile, "I'd advise you not to do it. I never knew anything by the name of Lincoln to amount to much."

He smiled then. But there were many days when that dark thought haunted him and drove him into depths of gloom and desperate melancholy. Was there, after all, no hope for him? No bright future ahead?

Here was Stephen A. Douglas, now a famous Senator, chairman of the very important committee dealing with new territories, and spoken of as a future President.

And he, Abraham Lincoln, what was he? Still a poor country lawyer, practically unknown outside of his own state.

PRESIDENT

One spring day when Lincoln was in one of the small towns out on the circuit, news came from Washington that Senator Stephen A. Douglas was coming home to Illinois. That famous Senator, now spoken of by his good friends as "The Little Giant," was coming to explain to his good friends about a certain law. It was a law concerning slavery passed by Congress in 1854, shortly before Kansas was ready to become a state. Senator Douglas himself had proposed the law and thought it was a very good one.

Lincoln did not agree with him. All that spring evening he and the other lawyers sat in the Judge's little hotel bedroom discussing the new law and the whole dreadful question of slavery, which seemed to be never-ending.

Every time a new state was to be added to the Union, the question came up again. When all of the United States lay east of the Mississippi, it had not been hard to settle. Then the Ohio River had divided the slave states from the free. All Congress had to do, as new states came in, was to be sure to keep the number of slave and free states equal.

But now the United States had spread beyond the Mississippi (where the Ohio ended) and the old dividing line was gone. So now, when the question came up, it was more difficult to handle. Each time, Congress tried to satisfy both those who wanted more slave states and those who did not. The result was that nobody was satisfied, and Congress was to blame.

"Therefore," said Mr. Douglas, "why should Congress worry about it any longer? Let the people of each new state decide for themselves whether it shall be a slave state or a free state." That was the new law.

And it had been tried out in what was now called "bloody Kansas" because of the fighting and bloodshed it had caused among the Kansas settlers. The same thing would happen, Lincoln said, wherever it was tried.

Long after the other lawyers had left the room, Lincoln kept on talking and thinking about it, until the Judge had fallen sound asleep. But Lincoln could not sleep. Hour after hour, he sat on the edge of the bed in his long, yellow night-shirt, turning the problem over and over in his mind, studying it from every angle.

How the awful question of slavery could finally be settled, he did not know. But he did know that the nation could not go on forever HALF slave and HALF free. It would have to be all one thing, or all another. There was no use trying to dodge the question any longer. It had to be asked and answered.

As dawn came creeping in through the window, Abraham Lincoln had made the great decision that was the turning point in his life.

He challenged Stephen A. Douglas to defend the law he had supported, in a series of debates.

Mr. Douglas did not hesitate to accept the challenge. What had he to fear from this old rival who had fallen so far behind him in the game of politics?

The debates took place in the summer of 1858, in seven little towns in Illinois. Each debate brought the excitement of the people to a higher pitch. Crowds came in clouds of dust from all over the surrounding prairie—on foot, on horseback, by ox team and stagecoach. And by the new railroad, as far as it went. That's the way the Honorable Mr. Douglas traveled, as a guest of the railroad. Lincoln got from town to town any way he could.

At each town, bands were playing, peddlers were selling souvenirs, and the crowd milling about, waiting to see Douglas, "The Little Giant," meet Honest Abe, "The Giant Killer," in a wrestling match of words. Onto the wooden platform, draped in red white and blue, would step the two contestants, the one so very short, followed by the one so very tall.

First Mr. Douglas would step forward, acknowledge the applause with a graceful gesture. Then he would throw back his head, and let the words pour forth—creamy, smooth-flowing, high-sounding words. Words in which he was careful to say nothing about slavery that could offend anyone who might vote for him in the next election. That's what he was thinking of.

Then Abraham Lincoln would unfold his long legs and step forward. His voice, at first, sounded high and thin. But the words he spoke were plain simple words that anyone could understand. They were strong, straightforward, honest words that struck squarely at the question of slavery. Slavery, that was tearing the United States apart. To save the Union, that was what he was thinking of, not what happened to himself.

As Douglas listened, he was first amazed, then startled, angry and alarmed. He felt himself being cornered, caught and pinned down by one direct question, which he could not wriggle out of. Yet he could neither answer "YES" or "NO," without offending one half of the Democratic party. He dared not offend his own Democrats in the free state of Illinois, so, with one word, he lost the support of all the southern Democrats who believed in slavery.

The complete story of these Lincoln-Douglas Debates was printed in newspapers all over the country.

"Who is this man Abraham Lincoln, out there in Illinois?" people began to ask. They wanted to hear him speak. Invitations came to him from as far away as New York City.

And now a new REPUBLICAN party, formed by

those who wished to stop the spread of slavery, had taken the place of the old Whigs. And in 1860, this new Republican party nominated Abraham Lincoln as its candidate for President. Fence rails he had split were carried to the convention which was held in Chicago. More rails were bundled up and shipped all over the country, as soon as the campaign was on to make "Honest Abe, the Rail Splitter," President. And when returns came in, on November 4th, he had won the election!

Stephen A. Douglas was defeated because the southern Democrats had broken away and supported another man. It was like the bundle of sticks, in an Aesop's fable, that could not be broken until it was divided. If the Democratic party had not been split in two, it would have been strong enough to win.

Now the country was in an uproar. The southern Democrats were furious that what they called a "Black Republican" had been elected President. The southern states threatened to secede from the Union if he ever lived to take the oath of office on the 4th of March. Letters came to

Lincoln threatening to kill him if he ever dared to leave Springfield for Washington. To Lincoln those four months of waiting, from November to March, seemed endless.

But not to Mrs. Lincoln. Four months were none too long to order all the new gowns and bonnets and shawls, feathers and roses to wear, at last, in the White House in Washington!

In January, Lincoln went down state to see an old lady, to look into her eyes, and feel her arms about him, just once more. His father was dead, but his "best friend," Sarah Bush Lincoln, was still living in the old log cabin. And how happy she was to see her "boy" again—but sad, too. Somehow, in her heart, she knew it would be for the last time.

The day before he left Springfield, Lincoln went to the law office to say goodbye.

"Billy," he said, "let the old sign hang undisturbed. If I ever come back, we'll go on again just where we left off."

Finally, the February morning came and the hour to leave. There were five of them. Robert, now eighteen, was going east to enter Harvard.

The two little boys were going to Washington. William was eleven, and Tad (short for Tadpole) was eight. His real name was Thomas.

It was a drizzly, cold morning. Fog and smoke from the funnel-shaped stack of the small engine hung low over the crowd gathered at the railroad station. In his high black hat, with a shawl about his shoulders, Lincoln stood on the back platform. As he looked down upon the friendly faces, words came from his heart:

"My friends," he said, "no one can appreciate my feeling of sadness at this parting. To this place and the kindness of these people, I owe everything. . . . I now leave . . . with a task before me greater than that which rested upon Washington. . . . Trusting in Him who can go with me and remain with you, and be everywhere for good, let us confidently hope that all will yet be well. To His care commending you, as I hope in your prayers you will commend me, I bid you an affectionate farewell . . ."

The train whistled. It began to move. The tall dark figure on the platform grew smaller and smaller, and disappeared into the fog.

CALIFORN
Territo
NEWORL
CONFE

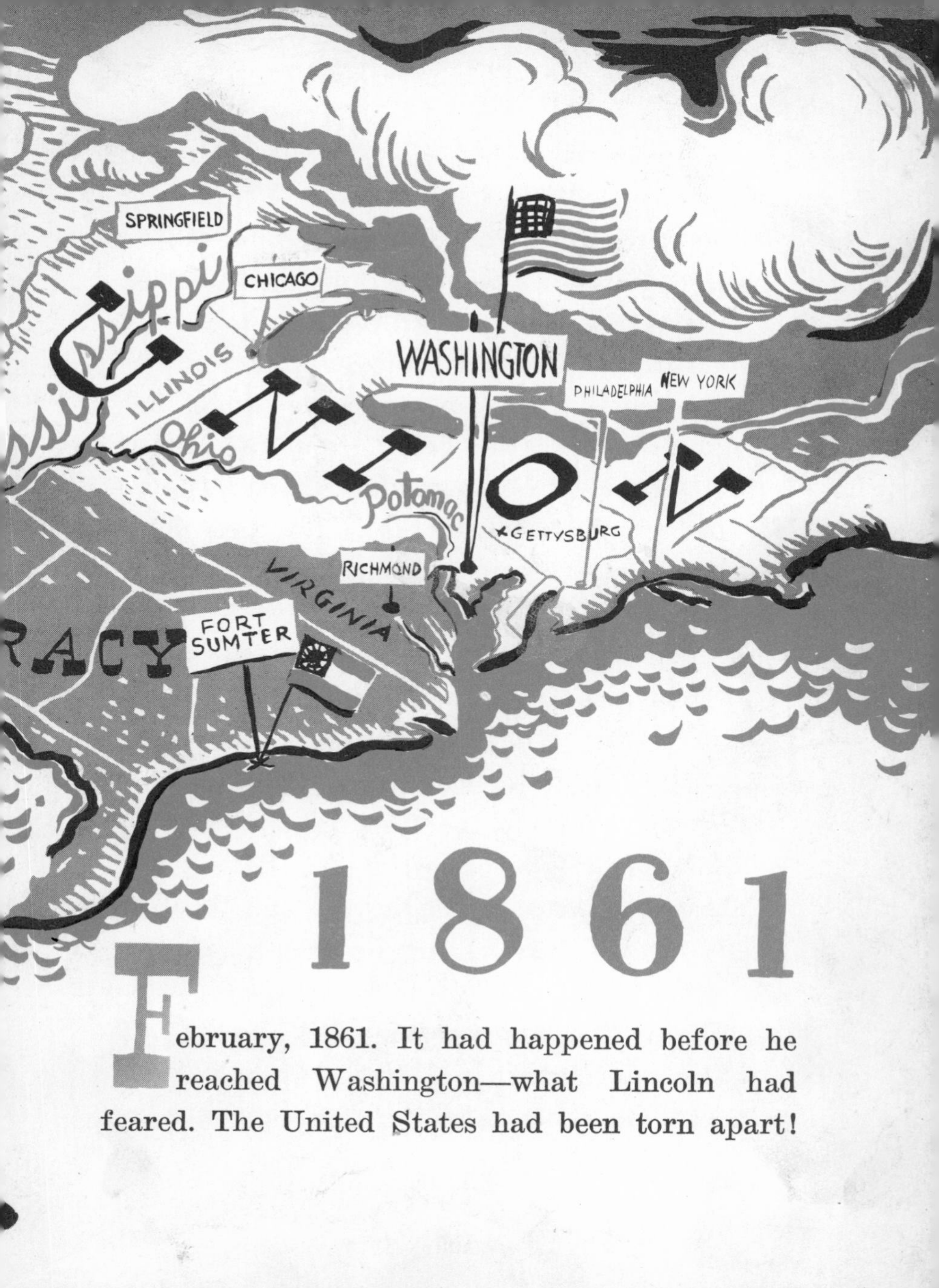

1861

February, 1861. It had happened before he reached Washington—what Lincoln had feared. The United States had been torn apart!

South Carolina and six other southern states had seceded. They had elected a President, Mr. Jefferson Davis, and formed a new nation of their own, the Confederate States of America.

There had been so many threats to take Lincoln's life that soldiers were on guard in Washington, all along the way, on the day of his inauguration. At the Capitol building, itself, a soldier stood at every window. Fifty armed men were stationed beneath the flag-draped platform on which the ceremony took place.

Mr. Buchanan, the outgoing President, walked to his seat with other government officials, nervous and shaken. Lincoln appeared calm. His only concern, as he rose to speak, seemed to be where to set his high black hat. Someone behind him took it and held it for him. It was Stephen A. Douglas.

Lincoln spoke especially to his "dissatisfied countrymen," urging them to think calmly, not to act in haste. "There will be NO WAR," he said in closing, "unless *you* start it."

The chief justice rose then, old and bent, and opened the Bible. Lincoln raised his right hand

and repeated after him these serious words:

"I do solemnly swear that I will faithfully execute the office of PRESIDENT OF THE UNITED STATES, and will, to the best of my ability, preserve, protect and defend the Constitution of the United States."

That vow, now taken by the 16th President, had been repeated for the first time by George Washington. Then the 13 states had just been united into a new nation. Now that nation, numbering 34 states, was being torn apart.

Would this new President be able to save the great Union? Would he have the courage and faith to protect, preserve and defend it as he had just promised to do? That was the awful task that now rested upon Abraham Lincoln.

After the ceremony, the family rode down Pennsylvania Avenue to the White House, where Mr. Buchanan introduced them to the staff.

Once inside the door, Tad and Willie went wild, running up and down stairs from the top floor to the basement. They interviewed every servant, secret service man, messenger and watchman. They ran to the conservatory to look at the lily tank and the goldfish. They dashed upstairs into every room, bounced on the beds and turned somersaults. They slid down the banisters, and then ran upstairs again, to get their father to play leapfrog with them down the hall.

"Paw won't have time to play with us to-night," said Willie. "He's going to the Ball."

"Yes, he will," said Tad running into his father's office and jumping into his lap. "Who's that?" he asked, pointing to an old portrait above the marble fireplace.

"Andrew Jackson—and badly cracked, too," answered Mrs. Lincoln. She had been on a tour of the whole house. The entire place, she said, was in bad repair. The carpets were filthy. Tomorrow she'd have them all ripped up and burned and order new carpets and furniture.

At her first Ball that night, the wife of the new President wore her blue satin gown with ostrich feathers in her hair.

Mr. Lincoln wore white kid gloves, shook hands for two hours, led the grand march, but did not dance. Stephen A. Douglas danced the quadrille with Mary Todd Lincoln.

Bad news came to President Lincoln the next morning—his first day in office.

At Fort Sumter, a United States fort off the coast of South Carolina, the food supply had been cut off, with only enough left for about a month.

On April 12, the fort was fired upon, and captured the next day by South Carolina soldiers.

The United States flag came down.

The Confederate flag went up.

WAR HAD BEGUN!

With a sad heart, Lincoln sent out a call for 75,000 soldiers to defend the Union.

Soon four more southern states seceded, and their capital was moved to Richmond, Virginia, for Virginia had now joined the Confederacy. There, just over the Potomac River from Washington, the Confederate flag was flying and Confederate soldiers were gathering.

Standing in the south window of his office, Lincoln could see across the river with his spyglass. How he hoped and prayed that some of those 75,000 soldiers he had called for would soon come to protect the city! Day after day passed and they did not come. Then they could not. The railroads were torn up. Trains were not coming in. Telegraph wires were cut. Washington was completely isolated and unguarded. Lincoln was nearly frantic. Any day he feared to see Confederate soldiers marching on the long bridge over the Potomac.

"Let 'em come!" cried Tad, rushing through the office with a broom for a gun. "We've got a fort up on the roof, Willie and me. Let 'em come! Willie and me are ready for 'em."

Lincoln smiled. But at night he paced the floor, praying for those northern soldiers. Finally they began to trickle in, just a few at first. Then more and more companies came marching by—marching by—marching by. All night long, their cannon and battery could be heard rumbling down the street. By the end of May, they were in Virginia, camped at the other end of the long bridge. And northern newspapers were screaming for them to "GO ON TO RICHMOND!"

Richmond was one hundred miles away.

The soldiers were not trained or ready. But on July 21, they advanced twenty miles and fought the Confederate soldiers at a little creek called BULL RUN. It was Sunday. From Washington, sightseers drove over to view that first battle as if it were a horse-race or a tournament. About noon, Willie and Tad from their roof-top fort, heard the cannon booming like the slamming of big doors. From noon on, Lincoln was listening in the telegraph office of the War Department. The news was so good that about five o'clock he went for a short drive to rest. An hour later, he was met at the door of the White House by his two secretaries, who said there had been a bad defeat. In a short time, sightseers were streaming in to report the disaster. Panic-stricken, they were certain that any moment the rebel army would be in Washington. All would be lost!

The next day the newspapers were blaming the defeat on the stupid government, the good-for-nothing President, "ignoramus and imbecile!"

Lincoln, being President of the United States in time of war, was, therefore, the Commander-in-Chief. As such, he realized that he needed to learn more about military tactics. So he did as he had always done. He got books and read and

GENERAL GRANT AT A RECEPTION IN THE ROOM MARKED "E"
Emancipation Proclamation
WHIT

C
E
E
E
CABINET MEMBERS MET IN THE ROOM MARKED "C"
GETTYSBURG ADDRESS
HOUSE

studied every moment that he could crowd into his busy day. Before long, his generals were amazed at how well he understood their needs and problems.

By fall, Tad and Willie were also studying, or supposed to be. Their mother had engaged a tutor for them. Desks and a blackboard had been set up in the State dining room.

But how could two little boys study, when ponies, rabbits, goats, and all kinds of pets were constantly being sent to them as presents?

Willie had a pony that he loved. He insisted on riding it one cold, drizzly February day, much like the one on which they had left Springfield the year before. He caught cold and became very ill, grew worse day by day, and in an almost unbelievably short time he died.

Poor little Tad couldn't—wouldn't—believe it. His mother was almost beside herself with grief. Lincoln tried his best to comfort both of them. But at night, the guard outside of his door heard the sad man pacing the floor, or moaning in his sleep.

And so ended their first year in the White House.

EMANCIPATION

Freeing of the slaves was the truly great event in Abraham Lincoln's second year as President. A few days after Willie's funeral, he called a meeting of his Cabinet to discuss the problem of how to go about it. For many months, he said, he had been trying to think of a plan for freeing the slaves that would be fair and just to their owners.

Cabinet meetings were held in the White House in a room which the President entered from his office. As he started to speak, the seven members of the Cabinet were seated with him around a long table. All wore beards except Mr. Seward, the Secretary of State, a tall man, with thick, iron-gray hair and a very large nose. Mr. Stanton, Secretary of War, had the longest beard of all, the greatest amount of energy, and the least patience.

He was forever in a fret to get back to his important business in the War Department. As to freeing the slaves, his one idea was not HOW to do it, but to DO it, and be done with it. To his mind, this discussion abut being fair to their owners was a useless waste of time. And it didn't help his temper to have the meeting prolonged and interrupted by a loud thump on the door.

After the thump came a short, sharp rap. Then a slow thump. Then another slow thump and two sharp raps. Mr. Lincoln listened and smiled.

"— T, . — A, — . . D. That's Tad," he said, rising. "I promised always to answer him when he used the Morse code."

He opened the door.

In rushed Tad, like a small cyclone, gave his father a big bear hug, scurried about for what he was after, and hurried out again, calling back that he "wanted to go along to the telegram office when the meeting was over."

The telegraph office was on the second floor of the War Department, across the lawn from the White House. There Lincoln spent part of every day, listening to reports that came in from the armies and generals at the front.

Usually he walked over the last thing at night before he went to bed. Often Tad went with him. Stanton would see them coming—the tall man and the small boy—walking hand in hand along the gravel path.

There were now two Union armies in the field, the one here in the east on the Potomac River, another out west on the Mississippi. Occasionally a bit of good news ticked in from the army in the west. From there, on February 6th, had come the first report of a Union victory. A battle had been won by an unknown general, by the name of Grant, whose initials happened to be the same as those of the United States, and also of the terms he had demanded after that victory: Unconditional Surrender—U. S. Grant.

There was no good word from the Army of the Potomac. Week after week, men, supplies, horses and ammunition were sent, but the army was bogged down. By the end of May, they were ten miles from Richmond, and could get no farther.

For the great General Robert E. Lee, of Virginia, was now in command of the army defending the Confederate capital. In June, he attacked the Union army and drove them back in a horrible battle lasting seven days!

Reports of the dead and wounded were sickening. Each despatch that came in tore at Lincoln's heart, as if each soldier that died had been his own son. Boys in blue uniforms or gray, it did not matter. He could hardly endure it. They were all part of his family.

One day, as he came sadly in to the telegraph office, he asked for a few sheets of paper.

"I want to write something special," he said, "that *may* help to end this war. I can work more quietly here than in the White House."

He sat down at a desk by the window. "But he did not write much at once," the chief operator said, in telling of it later. "He would look out of the window and study between times. . . . Once his eye rested on a large spiderweb stretched from the portico to the outer window sill." He was much interested when "a big spider soon appeared at the crossroads, tapped several time on the strands, whereupon five or six others came for a confab."

Lincoln came each day to write. When he was ready to leave, he asked the operator to take care of what he had written, and let no one see it.

When he had finally finished, he said,

"I have written an order, giving freedom to the slaves in the south."

At the next Cabinet meeting he read what he had written. All agreed that the order should be issued. But Secretary Seward felt that this was not the time to do it, saying:

"I think it would be wiser to wait until after a Union victory." Again they agreed.

So Lincoln waited for a victory. No victory came. Instead, another defeat at the end of August—the second Battle of Bull Run. And things grew darker than ever. General Lee crossed the Potomac, above Washington, and was marching north through Maryland toward Philadelphia. There he was finally stopped the middle of September by the Union army at a spot called Antietam Creek. There, after one of the bloodiest battles of the war, the boys in gray were driven back. The time had come.

One week later, Lincoln called a Cabinet meeting. Mr. Stanton came tearing in, beard and coat-tails flying—no time to waste. All the men were tense and nervous from the strain of the past weeks. Lincoln adjusted his glasses, and opened—

not a paper, as they had expected—but a small battered book, saying:

"Gentlemen, let me read you a chapter in this book that is very funny." He laughed when he had finished and looked about. One or two smiled faintly. Stanton, not at all. "Can't you laugh?" said Lincoln, gently. "You all need to as much as I. Under this awful strain, I should die if I could not laugh."

Then his face grew grave, the tone of his voice changed as he said: "The time has come now, I believe, to issue the order setting free the slaves. I shall read it to you again." He unfolded the paper and read the words written in the telegraph office, stopping often to comment as he went along. The order stated that:

On January 1, 1863, all slaves in states STILL AT WAR with the United States would then, henceforth and forever be free.

Four months passed. The states were still at war. The choice had been made.

New Year's Day came. January 1, 1863. And with it, the annual New Year's Day reception in the East Room of the White House. Lincoln

ONE LAST POSE

stood shaking hands with the guests until mid-afternoon. Then he was told that the Secretary of State was waiting for him in his office. Mr. Seward had brought the final order, copied on parchment, for the President to sign.

"My hand is stiff from shaking hands all morning," said Lincoln, as he took up his pen, "I hope my writing does not tremble. I would not want anyone to say that I hesitated to sign my name to this paper. For I never, in all my life, felt more certain that I was doing right."

So he dipped his pen and wrote his name

Abraham Lincoln.

thus signing what was called the

PROCLAMATION OF EMANCIPATION

Two years later, it was made a law by Congress that slavery should exist no longer *anywhere* in the United States. That law was added to the Constitution as the 13th Amendment. So by law, at least, the words of the Declaration of Independence had finally been made good.

All citizens of the United States had equal right to Life, Liberty and the Pursuit of Happiness.

AT GETTYSBURG

Only one of the battles in this sad war between the states was fought on northern soil. That took place in July, 1863, just over the Pennsylvania state line, near the little town of Gettysburg. The fighting lasted three days. When it was over, when the cannons were still and the smoke had cleared away, more than 40,000 men and boys in gray and blue uniforms lay dead on the battlefield. On November 19th, four months later, a ceremony was held to dedicate that field as a National Cemetery.

A special train left Washington the day before. As Lincoln stepped aboard, he carried, either in his high hat or in his pocket, a sheet of White House stationery. On this the short speech he was to make was partly written. He had been asked to make it brief. Mr. Edward Everett, for many years famous as an orator, was to make the principal address.

A flag-draped platform had been erected on the battlefield. Mr. Everett spoke two hours. His speech was learned and polished, but it has long been forgotten. After he finished, the band played a selection. Then Lincoln rose.

The words he spoke took but a few short moments, but they will be remembered as long as the English language is spoken. They were so simple and so beautiful.

"Four score and seven years ago, our fathers brought forth on this continent a new nation, conceived in liberty and dedicated to the proposition that all men are created equal.

"Now we are engaged in a great civil war, testing whether that nation, or any nation so conceived and so dedicated, can long endure.

"We are met on a great battlefield of that war. We have come to dedicate a portion of that field as the final resting place of those who here gave their lives that that nation might live. It is altogether fitting and proper that we should do this.

"But in a larger sense we cannot dedicate, we cannot consecrate, we cannot hallow this ground. The brave men, living and dead, who struggled here, have consecrated it far above our poor power to add or detract. The world will little note, nor long remember, what we say here, but it can never forget what they did here.

"It is for us the living, rather to be dedicated here to the unfinished work which they who fought here have thus far so nobly advanced. It is rather for us to be here dedicated to the great task remaining before us, that from these honored dead we take increased devotion to that cause for which they gave the last full measure of devotion; that we here highly resolve that these dead shall not have died in vain; that this nation, under God, shall have a new birth of freedom

and that government
of the people, by the people and for the people
shall not perish from the earth."

TOWARD THE END

President Lincoln was ill on his return from Gettysburg. Fortunately, he was soon up and at his desk again. But he looked gray and worn and so tired that his friends urged him to rest. He only smiled and shook his head.

"I can't rest," he said. "The tired part of me is *inside,* out of reach."

There could be no rest until the war was over. The number of problems he had to meet, the number of questions he had to answer, the amount of abuse he had to endure were endless. Day after day, he was besieged by visitors, bringing all kinds of complaints and suggestions. Throngs filled the corridor, waiting their turn to be admitted to his office.

One day as the door opened, Lincoln had a happy surprise. A wiry, little old fellow just stood there, and said, "Howdy, Abe."

"Dennis! Dennis Hanks!" cried Lincoln. For this was the one who had paid him his first visit, fifty-five years ago, and been so disappointed. Lincoln threw his arms about him and asked all about the Johnsons and Hankses, and later gave him a silver watch to take home for a keepsake. He was always so glad to see his old friends from Illinois and Indiana. He often thought he would like to see Austin again, his first playmate in Kentucky.

Also, as the year 1864 began, Lincoln looked forward to meeting a man from Illinois. This man was not a friend, nor exactly a stranger. He was a major general in the army—the general who had won the first Union victory. Now he had captured the last fort on the Mississippi, and so ended the long campaign to gain control of the Mississippi River.

General Ulysses S. Grant. At the end of February, he was on his way to Washington to receive a new commission, and be given the supreme command of the Union armies. Lincoln had sent for him, and was expecting him.

The night Grant arrived, he went directly to the White House. To his dismay, it was the night of the President's reception. He was so shy, he wanted to turn back, but he couldn't do that. It was bad luck. So he threw away his cigar and

FRASER VALLEY UNION LIBRARY
J 93223
B
Li

went in. A short, seedy man, with a stubbly brown beard and a wrinkled uniform, he looked more like a man out of a job than a conquering hero. But the crowd knew him at once. He had barely spoken to Lincoln when someone cried, "Stand up, where we can see you!"

So, after Grant had been introduced to Mrs. Lincoln, he had to step up on one of the crimson sofas. There he stood, in his dusty boots, too embarrassed to say a word.

Yet this was the man who was to bring the war to an end with the capture of Richmond, the Confederate capital, and the surrender of that great and brave Virginia general, Robert E. Lee.

Before the end of March, Grant had gone across the Potomac and set up his headquarters with the Union army in Virginia. In May, he started southeast toward Richmond. From then on, he kept on. And, he said in a telegram,

"I intend to fight it out on this line, if it takes all summer." Which he did.

He was forced by his opponents to change his direction once or twice, but he *never* turned back. He kept on. And it took all summer, all fall, all winter, until spring came again. Then General Lee was obliged to surrender what was left of his constantly dwindling army.

The strain on Lincoln became almost unbearable as he read the lists of the dead and visited the wounded in the hospitals.

"I have a feeling," he said, "that I shall not live long after this war is over." That did not seem to worry him, however, nor did the eighty or more letters he had received threatening to kill him. "A man can die but once," he said, "but to live in constant fear of death is to die over and over again."

He only hoped that he might live to finish the task he had begun, and that the people would have faith enough in him to re-elect him in November. And they did, in spite of the fact that his critics blamed him, unfriendly newspapers printed ugly cartoons of him, and called him liar, thief, monster, fiend, tyrant, scoundrel, and long-armed gorilla. The people re-elected him. And he was grateful.

On March 5, 1865, the day of his second inauguration, he was almost happy. For then the end of the war was practically in sight. Just one month later, on April 9th, at 4:30 P.M. this long-awaited telegram came from Grant:

"General Lee surrendered the Army of Virginia this afternoon."

The Union had been saved. The war was over.

Next morning, at dawn, a five-hundred-gun salute to victory boomed out over the Potomac. At breakfast, Lincoln was serenaded by government employees singing *The Star-Spangled Banner*. People cheering and singing crowded the streets and filled the White House lawn. The bands played. Tad ran up and down, waving a Confederate flag. The President appeared and spoke at an upstairs window.

"I see you have a band," he said, "and I propose that you now play *Dixie,* the song of the south, one of the best tunes I know." So the band played *Dixie* and then *The Star-Spangled Banner* again. After that they marched away to the *Battle Hymn of the Republic.*

That night, Abraham Lincoln must have slept well. Surely the guard outside his door could not have heard him moaning.

A few nights later, though, Lincoln himself heard the sound of moaning and sobbing. The corridor outside was dark and empty. No one was there. He followed the sound through the deserted hall, down the stairs, until he stood in the doorway of the East Room. In the center of the room was a coffin draped in mourning.

"Who is dead?" he asked.

"The President," said one of the guards. "He was killed by an assassin."

Lincoln moaned. The sound of his own voice woke him. He was there, in his room—in his big walnut bed. It had been a dream. Mrs. Lincoln wrung her hands in distress as he told her of it later, for she believed he could foresee in dreams what the future held. She begged him to be careful—not to go alone at night to the telegraph office, or at least, if he did, to carry a cane.

"Don't worry, Mother," he said gently. "God knows what is best. I think He will work this out all right, in His own good way and time."

Then he smiled. "But I'll carry the cane, if it makes you feel any easier."

THE LAST DAY

Friday, April 14, 1865, was the last day. It was a beautiful spring day. The early morning sun was streaming over the White House lawn as Lincoln stepped from his big walnut bed. The smell of blossoming lilacs came in through the window. Seven o'clock, his time for starting work, found him at his desk as usual. By eight o'clock he was ready for breakfast. This morning his son Robert was with him. Robert was then twenty-one, and had just come from camp in Virginia. He had with him a photograph to show his father. Lincoln studied it with grave interest, for it was that of a man for whom he held only the deepest respect, General Robert E. Lee.

At eleven came the Cabinet meeting, at which General Grant was to be present. He was to describe the surrender, which had been signed in the parlor of a small brick house at Appomattox Court House, in Virginia.

At the last moment, as usual, Secretary Stanton came dashing in, a roll of maps and papers under one arm. They were plans for the reconstruction of the south. His idea was to whip the southern states back into shape, and do it in short order.

Lincoln shook his head. The problem would be difficult, at best. It must be handled in a way that would be fair and just to all those who had suffered. This thought he had put into the words of his inauguration speech:

"With malice toward none, with charity for all, let us . . . bind up the nation's wounds and do all which may achieve and cherish a just and lasting peace. . . ."

He turned to General Grant. "What terms," he asked, "did you offer the common soldiers?"

"I told them," said Grant, "to go back to their homes and families, and they would not be molested if they did nothing more."

Lincoln nodded. His face lighted up. That was right. That was the way it should be.

As the meeting adjourned, the President turned to General Grant again.

"Mrs. Lincoln and I are pleased that you and Mrs. Grant are to be with us at the theatre this evening. The play, I understand, is an amusing comedy called *The American Cousin.*"

General Grant looked embarrassed. He and Mrs. Grant, he said, had their tickets and were leaving Washington on the evening train. There must have been some mistake.

Lincoln agreed, and bade him goodbye.

In the afternoon among other visitors who came to see the President was the mother of a young soldier who had been sentenced to death for desertion. Lincoln signed the pardon, as he was so ready to do, whenever mercy could be used to soften justice.

It was late afternoon when he and Mrs. Lincoln went for a short drive. The willows were green along the river, the dogwood was in blossom, the air was soft. And he said:

"I never felt so happy in my life."

And that was as it should be. His work was done. He had found the work that he was meant to do in life, and done it well. That is the highest happiness anyone can know.

For the theatre, that April evening, Mrs. Lincoln chose her sky-blue taffeta, and pinned a wreath of pink roses in her hair. Lincoln picked up his high black hat; drew a small, gray shawl about his shoulders. The carriage drove up before the White House portico. They stepped out into the misty night, and were off, riding down the cobblestones of Pennsylvania Avenue, toward Ford's Theatre, to see the celebrated comedy.

Also on his way to the theatre was a certain young actor by the name of John Wilkes Booth. He was to play a part that evening, not in the comedy, but in a tragedy of his own evil design.

The President's box, close to the stage, was draped in flags. As he entered with Mrs. Lincoln, the audience rose and cheered, and the band played *Hail to the Chief*. The Lincolns had as guests a young lady and a young Major by the name of Rathbone.

Lincoln sat in a rocking chair. He leaned forward, with his long arms folded on the rail to enjoy the play, and rocked back to visit happily during the intermissions.

The curtain went up for the third act. It was halfway through, when . . .

There was a shot.

A woman shrieked.

From the President's box a man swung himself

toward the stage, caught his heel in the flag, stumbled to his feet, flourished a dagger and dashed from the scene, shouting something about the death of "tyrants."

The audience rose in panic and confusion. What had happened? The President! He'd been shot? How? How could it happen? Where was the guard? Where was the President?

The crowd surged into the lobby, blocking the entrance to the box. They were pushed back to make way for the makeshift stretcher on which the tall man was carried out, wounded and unconscious. Blood from the back of his head fell in red drops on the white programs, scattered like dead leaves on the floor.

They took him to a small house, across the street, belonging to a tailor. Someone ran ahead and lighted the gas jet in a small room at the back. They laid him on a narrow bed.

The doctors came. But none could bring him back from the shadowy valley between life and death. At dawn, his breathing grew less regular, and by seven o'clock the tired part inside of him was gone.

For three days the long mirrors in the White House were dimmed with hangings of black and purple gauze, and his coffin stood as he had seen it in his dream.

This was no dream. This was the deep, dreamless sleep, the rest he had so rightly earned. For now, he too, had given the last full measure of devotion.

It was for those who lived—as it is for us the living—to see that they who died for freedom "shall not have died in vain, and that government of the people, by the people and for the people shall not perish from the earth."